# The <u>most</u> <u>excellent</u> book of
# face
# painting

*Margaret Lincoln*
*Illustrated by Rob Shone*

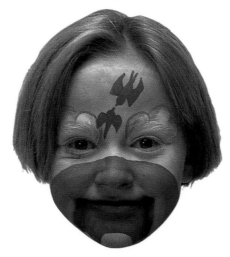

COPPER BEECH BOOKS
BROOKFIELD, CONNECTICUT

© Aladdin Books Ltd
1997
*Designed and produced by*
Aladdin Books Ltd
28 Percy Street
London
WIP 0LD

*First published in the
United States in 1997 by*
Copper Beech Books,
an imprint of
The Millbrook Press
2 Old New Milford Road
Brookfield, CT 06804

*Editor*
Sarah Levete
*Design*
David West
Children's Book Design
*Designer*
Rob Perry

*All faces painted by*
Margaret Lincoln, *except
for cover, top right* - Flick
Killerby.

Printed in Belgium
All rights reserved

Library of Congress
Cataloging-in-Publication Data
Lincoln, Margaret.
Face painting / by Margaret
Lincoln ; illustrated by Rob
Shone.
p. cm. — (Most excellent
book of—)
Includes index.
Summary: Designs for face
painting for all occasions,
decoration ideas, hints for
perfecting make-up skills, and
acting tips.
ISBN 0-7613-0551-3 (lib. bdg.). –
–ISBN 0-7613-0576-9 (pbk.)
1. Face painting—Juvenile
literature. [1. Face painting.]
I. Shone, Rob, ill- II. Title.
III. Series.
TT911.L56 1997     96-48466
745.5—dc21          CIP AC

# CONTENTS

# INTRODUCTION

Throughout history, people have painted their faces for different purposes. Iroquois Indians *(below left)* use paints to identify their tribe; actors in Chinese opera *(left)* and Indian Kathakali dancers *(below right)* use grease paint to make their characters appear fierce or beautiful. This book introduces you to professional face painting techniques. It uses special water-soluble face paint which is easier to apply and remove than grease paint.

As you read the book, look for these symbols:

★ shows what you need to complete your design.

✔ gives you tips on how to perfect your face painting and hints on acting out a character to suit your face.

Remember, practice makes perfect.

Have fun with your face!

# *Ready, set,* GO!

## Always use the proper equipment that is safe for faces.

Towel     Hairband

Mirror    Sponges

★ *What you need to buy: a selection of water-soluble face paints, which come either in small palettes or individual jars, face-painting sponges, and a selection of special face-painting brushes. Choose a fine, round brush, a medium flat brush, and a large round brush.*

You can buy these materials at a good craft or theatrical costume store. Only use materials that are specifically for use on the face. If you add glitter to a design, make sure it is special polyester glitter gel for face painting: Ordinary glitter is made of glass and could damage your model's skin or eyes.

★ *You will also need a water jar and shallow dish filled with some water, a jar to stand your brushes in, a hairband for your model's hair, and an old towel or shirt to protect your model's clothing.*

Flat brush

Round brush

Jars of paint

## Setting up

Set your equipment out on a table covered with an old cloth or towel to protect it from any spills. Make sure your model's face is clean. If your model has a face rash or cold sore, paint his or her hands and arms instead. If he or she has a skin allergy, apply some paint on his or her inside wrist. If there is no reation after an hour, you can paint his or her hand.

*Water jar and shallow bowl*

## Cleaning up

Wash your "face" off after a few hours. Use soap and water or baby wipes. Wash off any spills on clothes with cold water and then detergent. Use gentle soap flakes (not liquid or powdered detergent) to clean your equipment *(see pages 6-9)*.

*Always take care when painting close to the eyes.*

# *Sponging and* COLORING

## Many designs have a sponged base.

★ *If you can, use one sponge for each color, or wash your sponge out between each color. Practice stages 1-3 before you try the haunted forest base (yellow, orange, and burgundy).*

Orange

Burgundy

Yellow

4

5

**1** Dip the surface of the sponge into a bowl with some clean water in it. Squeeze as much of the water back out as you can, so the sponge is barely damp. Rub its wet side over your chosen color until it is covered in paint.

**2** Apply evenly, covering your model's face, so that no skin is showing. Be careful around the nose and eyes. Make sure the base doesn't end in a jagged edge on the outside.

**3** If your design blends two or more colors in bands, overlap each one slightly, rather than ending with one color and then starting the other next to it.

**4**  For the haunted forest base, use yellow, orange, and burgundy face paints, sponged in diagonal bands. The colors should merge gradually into each other.

**5**  Over the base, create amazing designs. For the haunted forest, use black and white face paints, a medium brush for the ghost, and a fine brush for the twigs.

## Color Crazy

Start with a small palette and build up your selection gradually. Experiment with different mixes, using different quantities of each color to alter the finished result. Try the rainbow sky *(right)*.

## Keeping clean

Change the water regularly in your jar to keep your paints clean. When you have finished painting, clean the surface of each paint block with a clean, wet sponge or tissue. Let the surface dry and replace the lids. Wash your sponges in warm, soapy water. Rinse them well in clean water and squeeze them out hard. Leave them to dry.

*Paint in rainbow sky detail.*

*Blend a white and blue base.*

# *Brush up your* STROKES!

## Clown around – and practice brushwork.

★ *Only use brushes recommended for face painting, because they won't prickle. Keep them separate from ordinary painting brushes so you don't mix them up. With a range of brushes you can paint everything from fine details to bold strokes, or you can use your brush to color in large areas of the design quickly. Try to think which size and shape of brush is most suitable for the effect you are trying to create.*

**1** Dip your brush into the clean water and tap it on the side of the jar to remove the drips.

*Use a flat brush on its side.*

**2** Hold your paint jar in your hand and rub your brush over the paint in a circular motion, until you've filled the brush with color.

*Use a fine brush*

✔ *On its broad side, use a flat brush to color in areas. On its thin side, use it to paint lines and strokes.*

**3** The more pressure you put on the brush, the thicker the line will be. Less pressure creates a finer line. To produce a tapered line, press harder for a thick line and then gradually lift the brush away.

**4** Try to paint your design with sweeping lines, rather than sketching gradually, as you would with a pencil.

**5** Practice your brush strokes to create some clown faces.

### Brush care

Wash your brushes in clean water before changing to a different color, or the paints will become "muddy." When you are not using them, stand your brushes with the bristle end upward in an empty jar, otherwise the tips will bend over. When you have finished painting, wash them in warm, soapy water, rinse well, and then leave your brushes bristle end upward in your jar.

*Sponge on a base color*

*Use a large brush to fill a large area*

# *Super*HERO

## Transform your friend into a superhero!

★ *Comic book characters are very easy to paint, even if you only have a limited selection of colors. For the following superheroes, all you need is one bright color, with black and white face paints, sponges, a wide flat brush, and a fine brush.*

**1** With your wide, flat brush, mark out a white "mouthpiece" and fill it in.

**2** With a bright color and wide flat brush, thickly outline the white. This will help you to keep the mouth area white so you won't have to sponge too close to it.

**3** Sponge the rest of the face with the bright color, avoiding the eye area.

*Cover the face evenly*

✔ *If the base is patchy, wet the corner of the sponge and squeeze it out. Apply more paint and dab it over the patchy areas. Be careful not to drag the sponge because this will take off the paint you have already applied.*

**4** Outline a black shape around the eyes.

**5** Add some details to make a "helmet."

**6** Fill in the eye area with black. Ask your model to shut his or her eyes so you can very gently color in this area.

**7** To make the helmet look more realistic and 3-D, add some shading to the helmet detail. To do this, make a gray color by mixing some black with a little of your bright color. With a wide brush, shade the area on one side of the helmet detail.

**8** Repeat this on the other side of the helmet.

4

6

7

8

✔ *Once you have created your superhero, why not make a costume to go with your new image? For a cape, use a piece of material to match your new face color. Now get going with some superhero deeds!*

5

# Comic CHARACTERS!

## Use simple shapes and colors to invent your own superheroes!

★ *You will need sponges, medium brush, yellow, black, and white face paints.*

**1** Sponge white shapes for your mask around the eyes.

**2** Sponge a yellow oval on the forehead.

**3** With your brush, outline the oval and the shape of the mask in black. Paint your own superhero image in the yellow area. Fill in the rest of the mask in black. Shade in some gray areas (black and white) to the jaw and chin.

✔ *If your sponged base becomes streaked, your sponge is probably too wet. Dab it on some paper towel to dry it off. Without adding water, rub more paint into it and go back over the streaked areas.*

★ *You will need sponges, medium and fine brushes, white, black, and red face paints.*

**1** Sponge in the white eye area.

**2** Use a brush to outline around this with red.

**3** Sponge the rest of the face in red.

**4** Use a very fine brush to paint a spider's web. It is difficult to paint straight lines, so take your time but be fairly bold in your strokes. Ask your model to be extra still. Paint the straight lines first, and then outline the eyes.

**5** Complete the web with some curved lines.

✔ *Practice drawing thin, straight brush lines on your own, or your model's hand. If you paint a line in the wrong place, don't panic – look at the mistake and see how you can use it to your advantage. If the face is meant to be symmetrical (the same on both sides), disguise the mistake by repeating it on the other side. No one will know!*

# *Tiger*, TIGER!

## Create your own fearsome tiger face.

★ *You will need sponges, medium and fine brushes, yellow, orange, red, white, and black face paints.*

**I** Sponge the whole face with yellow. Start from the center of the model's face, and work outward.

**2** Blend in a bright orange color around the edge of the face. Sponging a darker color around the edge will make your tiger look very realistic.

**3** Use a different sponge for the white muzzle shape.

✔ *Sponge different shades of color to give your faces depth. Use light colors, such as white, to highlight, bringing features forward. Darker colors make areas appear farther back.*

*If the design is lopsided, as here, correct it before you add the details by enlarging the small side.*

2

3

I

**4** Paint in spiked white eyebrows, starting at the nose and working outward and upward. Add some white stripes around the edge of the face.

**5** Paint a curved black line starting at the bridge of the nose, sweeping up and across, below the brow bone. Starting at the outer corner of the eye, paint a thin line, sweeping up from the outer corner of the eye to the end of the brow line.

**6** Add black stripes in the eyebrows and around the edge of the face.

**7** Paint a black nose and a line down the muzzle. Paint the top lip black; lengthen it, and make it sweep up at the ends.

**8** Use a fine brush to add whisker dots to each side of the muzzle. Paint the bottom lip red to complete the tiger.

✔ *For this face, roar and growl like a tiger! Use pictures and photos of real animals from other books to help you to create some other animal faces.*

# *Spotted* LEOPARD

Use the "tiger face" techniques *(see pages 14-15)* for the fanged leopard!

★ *You will need sponges, fine and medium brushes, yellow, orange, black, and white face paints.*

**1** Begin with the same steps as the tiger, but the muzzle goes above and below the lips. Paint a pair of "fangs" on the chin.

**2** Paint the top of the eye area white.

**3** Make the leopard spots by dabbing the brush onto the face. Make different-size spots by adding more or less pressure to the brush.

✔ *You can paint some leopard or tiger markings on your hands, too. All you need now is some fearsome animal noises to complete the transformation!*

# *Spectacled* MOUSE

## Are you really more afraid of mice than tigers or leopards ...?

★ *You will need sponges, fine and medium brushes, gray, pink, white, and black face paints.*

**1** Sponge the face white. Outline around the white with gray (mix black and white).

**2** Sponge in pink cheeks. Paint in fine black and white whiskers with a brush.

**3** Use a fine brush to draw the arched shape above each of the eyebrows. These will look like the ears of the mouse! Add some white details.

✔ *When you sponge, make sure that your model doesn't screw up his or her eyes, because this will crease the skin, and prevent the paint from covering the face evenly.*

# *Alien* INVASION

## How does it feel to be a Martian?

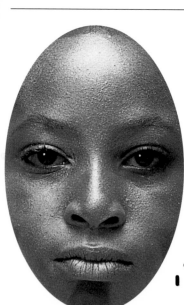

★ *For this Martian, you will need sponges, medium and fine brushes, bright green, dark green, white, black, and gold or yellow face paints.*

1 Sponge the whole face gold or yellow.

2 With a medium brush, mark out areas of Martian "flesh" in bright green. Try to make these areas as symmetrical as possible.

3 Fill in the fleshy areas, so that the center of the face looks like the Martian's shell, or outer casing.

4 To give the flesh some depth beneath the shell, shade the inner edges of the green areas with a little darker green. Blend this in with your finger or a clean, dry brush.

**5** With a fine brush, add skin texture by painting white "scales" in the green areas.

**6** Use a medium brush to paint black nostrils and "fangs." Leave a little of the base color showing through, to act as a highlight. To add to the effect, drape your model in a piece of colored material.

**6**

**5**

✔ To *create even more of an alien skin texture* (see page 21), *you can use the "stipple" technique. For this, you will need a stipple sponge or a new, dry nylon scouring pad. Press the stipple sponge onto the surface of your wetted paint and gently place it on your model's skin. The lighter the pressure, the more delicate the effect. When you stipple, it is important to avoid the eye area and not to press too hard anywhere on the face. Before you start on a face, practice on the back of your hand.*

# Creatures from SPACE

## Use your skills to create some weird space travelers!

★ *You will need sponges, a medium brush, white, black, and red face paints.*

**1** Sponge on a white base, then shade with some dark gray in the hollows of the cheeks and the forehead to give your model a bony "skull" shape. In black, outline some eye shapes.

**2** Paint in a row of black fangs and two horns on each side of the face. Leave a triangle of the white showing to highlight each fang. Outline the edges of the skull with soft red (mix in some white). Fill in the eye sockets with black and add some nostrils.

✓ *No one knows what an alien looks or sounds like – it's a perfect opportunity to let your imagination run away with you.*

★ *You will need sponges, a medium and fine brush, white, black, blue, and burgundy face paints.*

**1** Sponge the face white. Paint a thick blue line along the side of the nose and over the forehead. On both sides of the face, use the sponge to blend the blue paint into the white on the outer side of the line. Beneath the blue, paint a burgundy line, blend burgundy into the white.

**2** Paint a wavy blue line from the outer corner of the lips up to the hinge of the jaw. Blend upward into the white, using the same technique as before. Repeat with a burgundy line, blending the color downward.

**3** Stipple *(see page 19)* some white paint to add texture. Complete the face by painting the eyelids and nostrils.

*Stipple on white paint.*

*Add a symbol of your own.*

*Use a fine brush to dot the face with blue paint.*

# *Wizardly* TRICKS

## Be wise and wizardlike!

★ *You will need sponges, a fine and medium brush, black, lavender, purple, grey, and white or flesh-colored face paints.*

**1** Start by sponging on a white or flesh-colored base to cover the face. Then sponge lavender all around the outer edges of your model's face.

**2** Use a sponge to apply some gray down each side of the nose, in the eye sockets, temples, and hollows of the cheeks. Using a medium brush, paint in some white shaggy eyebrows.

**3** Paint in a white moustache and a beard.

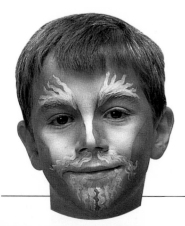

✓ *To give your wizard a more sinister look, choose some darker colors such as bright green shading and black eyebrows. With just a few brush strokes you can change the eyebrow and mouth shapes of the face which will dramatically alter your model's expression.*

**4** To make the face appear old and wise, use a fine brush with some dark gray paint to add some "wrinkles" around the eyes, mouth, nose, and lines on the forehead. This is one time when it helps to get your model to crunch up his or her face to show you where the wrinkles should go! Remember that if you don't have any dark gray paint, you can mix some white and black.

**5** Make the eyebrows and beard stand out more by adding some black wiggly lines.

**6** With a medium brush, paint the lips purple to complete the face.

✔ *Use some plain, dark fabric (old drapes are ideal) and make a simple hood. Why not decorate it by sewing on star and moon shapes cut from a light-colored fabric?*

# *Be a* DEVIL

Design a devilish demon.

★ *You will need a sponge, fine and medium brushes, red, black, and gold face paints.*

**1** Sponge the face bright red.

**2** To create a dramatic color, mix together a little red with some black. Test the color on your hand. Using this color, and black for the eyebrows, follow stage 2 for the wizard *(see page 22).*

**3** Paint gold horns, eyelids, and a mouth. With a fine brush, add black details on top.

**4** Dress the devil in a hood. Why not make a devil's fork out of cardboard.

# *Wicked* WITCH

## Cast a spell – turn your friend into a witch!

★ *You will need a sponge, fine and medium brushes, green, black, white, and red face paints.*

*Take extra care around the eyes*

**1** The green sponging here uses the same technique as for the Martian *(see pages 18-19).* Over the white base, paint some green lines from which you will sponge your green.

**2** Use a fine brush to paint black lines under the eyes; ask your model to look up when you do this. Add some witchlike details Redden the lips with a medium brush.

*Dress your witch in green material.*

✔ *Spook your friends with some witchy words to recite as you stir the secret potion in your cauldron.*

# *Creature features:* FROG

## "Ribet, ribet!"

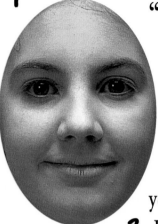

★ *You will need sponges, fine and medium brushes, white, yellow, green, red, black, and pink or orange face paints.*

**1** Sponge on a white base, blending yellow around the edge of the face.

**2** Blend some pink or orange over the eyelids and cheeks.

**3** With a fine brush, paint in the outline of the frog, marking out the position of the eyes and its underbelly.

**4** Fill in the rest of the shape with bright green. With a medium brush, strengthen the yellow of the frog's underbelly, painting it again; paint the eyes red, leaving a ring of white around them. Shade the top or the legs and the top of the head dark green.

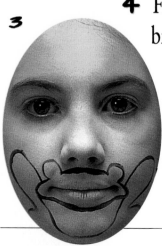

✔ *Make sure that you position and outline the frog's mouth directly over your model's lips, and position and outline the underbelly over the chin.*

**5** Finish the frog with red webbed toes and bottom lip.

**6** Paint stems around the face with a fine brush.

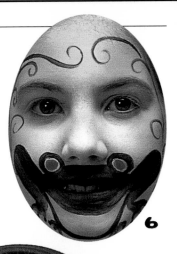

**7** Now add the leaves. Using a round, tapered brush makes them easy to paint by simply placing the the bristles down on the skin, tip first, pointing away from the stem.

**8** Add black pupils to the eyes, highlighted with a white dot. Add a dragonfly or other insect on one of the cheeks!

✔ *Have you ever heard a frog speaking like a human? Frogs make a sort of "ribet, ribet" noise.*
*Try it!*

# *Snappy* CROCODILE

## When your model smiles, the design is complete!

★ *You will need sponges, medium and fine brushes, bright and dark green, yellow, red, black, and white face paints.*

**1** Sponge on a white base with yellow and green shading. On one side of the face, paint some stems. With the tip of a fine brush toward the stem, add flowers and leaves with petals *(see page 31).*

**2** Outline the crocodile with its mouth over your model's mouth. Paint the top half of the body and legs in dark green. Leave the eyes and nostril white. Paint the underbelly bright green.

**2**

*Highlight with white.*

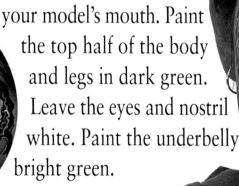

# *Creative* CRAB

## Create your own sea creatures.

★ *You will need sponges, fine and medium brushes, pale blue, pale green, orange, white, black, and pink face paints.*

**I** Paint in the crab on a blue and green base first. Fit the mouth of the crab over your model's mouth.

**2** Use your imagination to create your own underwater scene. Glitter will give your face a sparkly, watery look. Only use special polyester glitter gel that is safe for the skin. Apply it carefully with a brush or on your finger. Never apply it too close to the eyes.

✔ *Join with the frog and crocodile as you all snap, rivet, and crab around. Turn to page 31 for some handy tips to add to your gang of animals.*

# *Flower* POWER

## Practice this design on your hand first.

★ *You will need sponges, fine and medium brushes, yellow, orange, white, blue, purple, and green face paints.*

**1** Sponge on a white base. Blend in pale yellow around the edges and darker yellow over the eyelids and cheeks (mix yellow and orange). Practice flower and petal shapes on your hand first *(see opposite page)*. Use a medium round brush for your main flower in the middle of the forehead. Space a few others around the face.

*Add leaves to fill in any gaps.*

**2** Paint in some smaller flowers. Add a broken line, winding in and out of the design, as a ribbon trail. Paint some small flowers, at random between the larger ones. Paint the lips to finish the design.

1

2

# That's HANDY!

## Give us a hand...

✓ *If you can't paint your model's face or you want to paint yourself, why not paint hands, arms, or knees instead?*

Flower and leaf shapes are made simply by placing a round, tapered brush, tip first, down on the skin in patterns to make different arrangements of either pointed or rounded petals and leaves. Altering the pressure on your brush will make larger or smaller shapes. Practice some of these examples, and then experiment with your own ideas of shape and color. Look at some other books for pictures or photos of animals or insects that you can copy.

✓ *Use the techniques in this book to help you create your own fantastic faces. And don't forget to act the part!*

# *Face painting* WORDS

**Base** The background color or colors which cover the face.
**Blend** To merge two colors, using a sponge.

**Highlight** To draw attention to an area or detail, by adding a lighter color or white.
**Symmetrical** A shape or design that is exactly the same on both sides of the face.
**Water soluble** Paints that are mixed with and removed by water.

# *More* FACES!

Try creating your own designs. Keep a notebook of your ideas. Practice the techniques on your friends ... and keep having fun!

# INDEX

**Picture credits**
All photography by Roger Vlitos except for: page 3; Frank Spooner Pictures.